Gay Wit and Wisdom

Queer Quotes

From Your LGBT Family

To Make You Laugh and Think

by Cass Martinez

Gay Wit
and Wisdom

by Cass Martinez

There are several reasons some quotes stick with you:

Sometimes you hear someone say something and you think, "I know exactly what you mean."

Sometimes you hear someone say something and you think, "I've never thought of that before."

And there are times when you hear someone say something and think, "It was really important for me to hear that right now."

When I hear a quote like that, I write it down.

And, as a member of the queer family, hearing from other LGBTQI+ folks and allies is important; it's easy to feel alienated. So, in this book I've collected 100 quotations that I believe are significant - that make me feel connected.

Some come from activists and social justice warriors. Some come from celebrity icons. Some come from average people. But each quote has something important to say, and I'm privileged to share them with you.

Find a comfy place to sit. Relax. And enjoy.

Gay Wit and Wisdom

I hate the word homophobia. It's not a phobia. You're not scared. You're an asshole.
  - Morgan Freeman, American actor

The only queer people are those who don't love anybody.
  - Rita Mae Brown, American Feminist writer

The beauty of standing up for your rights is others see you standing and stand up as well.
  - Cassandra Duffy, American writer

Being gay is like glitter; it never goes away.

- Lady Gaga, American singer and actress

Gay people are the sweetest, kindest, most artistic, warmest and most thoughtful people in the world. And since the beginning of time, all they've ever been is kicked.

- Little Richard, American musical artist

I'm not missing a minute of this. It's the revolution!

- Sylvia Rivera, American drag queen and activist, during the Stonewall Riots

I would advise any gay person that being out - in the real sense - can never happen too soon.

- George Michael, English popstar

There's a Greek legend—no, it's in something Plato wrote—about how true lovers are really two halves of the same person. It says that people wander around searching for their other half, and when they find him or her, they are finally whole and perfect.

The thing that gets me is that the story says that originally all people were really pairs of people, joined back to back, and that some of the pairs were man and man, some woman and woman, and others man and woman.

What happened was that all of these double people went to war with the gods, and the gods, to punish them, split them all in two. That's why some lovers are heterosexual and some are homosexual, female and female, or male and male.

- Nancy Garden, American writer in her book "Nancy on My Mind"

Being a queer, black woman in America, someone who has been in relationships with both men and women – I consider myself to be a free-ass motherfucker.

- Janelle Monaé, American singer and actress

Queer people don't grow up as ourselves, we grow up playing a version of ourselves that sacrifices authenticity to minimise humiliation & prejudice. The massive task of our adult lives is to unpick which parts of ourselves are truly us & which parts we've created to protect us.

- Alexander Leon, English writer and activist

Jean is a nice person. She happens to like girls instead of guys. Some people like cats instead of dogs. Frankly, I'd rather live with a lesbian than a cat. Unless a lesbian sheds; that I don't like.

- Estelle Getty as Sophia Petrillo on The Golden Girls

Now that everyone knows, I have nothing to hide, those chains that I felt wrapped around me are gone, and I can carry on with my life as normal and be happy.

- Tom Daly, Olympic diver

The world is not divided into sheeps and goats. Not all things are black nor all things white. It is a fundamental of taxonomy that nature rarely deals with discrete categories. Only the human mind invents categories and tries to force facts into separated pigeon-holes. The living world is a continuum in each and every one of its aspects. The sooner we learn this concerning sexual behavior the sooner we shall reach a sound understanding of the realities of sex.

- Alfred Kinsey, sex researcher

Being born gay, black and female is not a revolutionary act. Being proud to be a gay, black female is.

- Lena Waithe, American actress and writer

Somebody, your father or mine, should have told us that not many people have ever died of love. But multitudes have perished, and are perishing every hour — and in the oddest places! — for the lack of it.

- James Baldwin, American novelist, playwright, poet and activist

I'm a supporter of gay rights. And not a closet supporter either. From the time I was a kid, I have never been able to understand attacks upon the gay community. There are so many qualities that make up a human being... by the time I get through with all the things that I really admire about people, what they do with their private parts is probably so low on the list that it is irrelevant.

- Paul Newman, American actor and philanthropist

Sweet mother, I cannot weave – slender Aphrodite has overcome me with longing for a girl.

- Sappho, Classical Greek poet

Girls love each other like animals. There is something ferocious and unself-conscious about it. We don't guard ourselves like we do with boys. No one trains us to shield our hearts from each other. With girls, it's total vulnerability from the beginning. Our skin is bare and soft. We love with claws and teeth and the blood is just proof of how much. It's feral. And it's relentless.

- Elliot Wake, Trans American author

Some people think I am gay, which I think is awesome.
- Daniel Radcliffe, English actor

Being gay is a natural normal beautiful variation on being human. Period. End of subject. Therefore, any argument which says differently is an immoral supremacist one. Call it out as such. ... Be outraged, offended, angry and intolerant of any discussion or any one who describes you as unequal, undeserving or unnatural for being just as you are.
- Larry Kramer, American author, playwright and activist

I just go crazy when I hear these people on the stages on gay pride rallies going on and on how "We're just like everyone else." Then a seven-and-a-half-foot drag queen comes walking by and opens his butterfly wings and I just think, "Yeah, we're just like everyone else." I think we should celebrate who we are. I don't need anyone's approval.

- Lea DeLaria, American actress and singer

Wherever it has been established that it is shameful to be involved with sexual relationships with men, that is due to evil on the part of the rulers, and to cowardice on the part of the governed.

- Plato, Ancient Greek philosopher

You could move.

- Abigail Van Buren, American advice columnist, Dear Abby, when she asked what could be down to improve the neighborhood now that gay people had moved in.

It is a tragedy, I feel, that people of a different sexual type are caught in a world which shows so little understanding for homosexuals and is so crassly indifferent to the various gradations and variations of gender and their great significance in life.

- Emma Goldman, political activist and writer

I hear the word "tolerance"—that some people are trying to teach people to be tolerant of gays. I'm not satisfied with that word. I am gay, and I am not seeking to be "tolerated". One tolerates a toothache, rush-hour traffic, an annoying neighbor with a cluttered yard. I am not a negative to be tolerated.

- Chely Wright, country music artist

You have the audacity to talk about protecting families and children from the homosexual menace, while you yourselves tear apart families and drive children to despair. I don't know why my son is gay, but I do know that God didn't put him, and millions like him, on this Earth to give you someone to abuse.

- Sharon Underwood, American comedian and host

Please remember, especially in these times of group-think and the right-on chorus, that no person is your friend (or kin) who demands your silence, or denies your right to grow and be perceived as fully blossomed as you were intended.
- Alice Walker, novelists essayist and activist

I've been embraced by a new community. That's what happens when you're finally honest about who you are; you find others like you.
- Chaz Bono, American activist

I learned compassion from being discriminated against. Everything bad that's ever happened to me has taught me compassion.
- Ellen Degeneres, American comedian and host

But I'm not a saint yet. I'm an alcoholic. I'm a drug addict. I'm homosexual. I'm a genius. Of course, I could be all four of these dubious things and still be a saint.
- Truman Capote, American writer, playwright and actor

I appeal to all governments and societies to promote the values of tolerance and respect for diversity, and to build a world where no one has to be afraid because of their sexual orientation and gender identity.

- António Guterres, UN Secretary-General

We're all just people made out of the same old dirt, and God didn't make any junk.

- Tammy Faye Bakker, American evangelist, talking about her gay friend Jim J. Bullock

Part of what my discomfort was, in the beginning, is that I wanted something that didn't exist. I wanted something that was so singular, a label that was so singular for me. I was so special—I was so different from everybody else I was meeting. And I wanted a different label. And I had to say, 'Charles, snap out of that. What are you talking about?' All identity labels are umbrella terms to some degree, but this term bisexual is not only serviceable but it is sufficient. And yes, it brings together a bunch of people who are maybe shades different from one another. And maybe that's the beauty of labels: that they force you to be with other people and see the difference.

- Charles M. Blow, American journalist

I was not ladylike, nor was I manly. I was something else altogether. There were so many different ways to be beautiful.
- Michael Cunningham, American novelist

Like racism and all forms of prejudice, bigotry against transgender people is a deadly carcinogen. We are pitted against each other in order to keep up from seeing each other as allies. Genuine bonds of solidarity can be forged between people who respect each other's differences and are willing to fight their enemy together. We are the class that does the work of the world, and can revolutionize it. We can win true liberation.
- Leslie Feinberg, Author and transgender activist

Um... I do drink red wine. But I also drink white wine.

And I've been known to sample the occasional rosé. And a couple summers back, I tried a merlot that used to be a chardonnay...which got a bit complicated.

I like the wine and not the label. Does that make sense?

- David Rose, as written and played by Canadian series creator Dan Levy on Schitt's Creek

The heterosexuals who hate us should just stop having us.

- Lynda Montgomery, American comedian

I have no idea why gay men love me, but I would have to assume it's because they know how much I love the gays! Everyone needs a good gay man in their life.

- Chelsea Handler, American TV host and writer

It is revolutionary for any trans person to choose to be seen and visible in a world that tells us we should not exist.

- Laverne Cox, American actress and trans activist

The pressures on gay teens can be overwhelming–to keep secrets, tell lies, deny who you are, and try to be who you're not. Remember: you are special and worth being cared about, loved, and accepted just as you are. Never, ever let anyone convince you otherwise.

- Alex Sanchez, American author of gay-themed novels for teens

That nothing here is promised, not one day. And love is love is love is love is love is love is love is love cannot be killed or swept aside. Now fill the world with music, love and pride.

- Lin-Manuel Miranda, American writer, composer, actor and poet

It may be that same-sex couples will save the institution of marriage.
- Elizabeth Gilbert, American Author and speaker

So let me be clear: I'm proud to be gay, and I consider being gay among the greatest gifts God has given me.
- Tim Cook, CEO of Apple

I've always known I was gay, but it wasn't confirmed until I was in kindergarten. It was my teacher who said so. It was right there on my kindergarten report card: PAUL IS DEFINITELY GAY AND HAS VERY GOOD SENSE OF SELF.
- David Levithan, American young adult author, in his book "Boy Meets Boy."

To regret one's own experiences is to arrest one's own development. To deny one's own experiences is to put a lie into the lips of one's own life. It is no less than a denial of the soul.
- Oscar Wilde, 19th Century Irish wit, poet and dramatist

The next time you hear a person say, "It's Adam and Eve, not Adam and Steve," reply with "It's homo sapiens not hetero sapiens," and fly into the night.
- Unknown

When I was dating a guy I was hiding everything that I did because everything personal felt like it was immediately trivialized, so I didn't like it. We were turned into these characters and placed into this ridiculous comic book, and I was like, 'That's mine. You're making my relationship something that it's not.' I didn't like that. But then it changed when I started dating a girl. I was like, 'Actually, to hide this provides the implication that I'm not down with it or I'm ashamed of it, so I had to alter how I approached being in public. It opened my life up and I'm so much happier.

- Kristen Stewart, American actress

I've struggled enough in my life to be appreciated and understood. I've had to go against all kinds of people through the years just to be myself. I think everybody should be allowed to be who they are, and to love who they love. I don't think we should be judgmental. Lord, I've got enough problems of my own to pass judgment on somebody else.

- Dolly Parton, country music artist and philanthropist

If I wait for someone else to validate my existence, it will mean that I'm shortchanging myself.

- Zanele Muholi, South African artist and activist

All of us who are openly gay are living and writing the history of our movement. We are no more — and no less — heroic than the suffragists and abolitionists of the 19th century; and the labor organizers, Freedom Riders, Stonewall demonstrators, and environmentalists of the 20th century. We are ordinary people, living our lives, and trying as civil-rights activist Dorothy Cotton said, to "fix what ain't right" in our society.

- Tammy Baldwin, the first openly gay US Senator

The richness, beauty and depths of love can only be fully experienced in a climate of complete openness, honesty and vulnerability.

- Anthony Venn Brown, activist and survivor of "conversion therapy"

It takes some intelligence and insight to figure out you're gay and then a tremendous amount of balls to live it and live it proudly.
- Jason Bateman, actor

Equality means more than passing laws. The struggle is really won in the hearts and minds of the community, where it really counts.
- Barbara Gittings, American activist

The Bible contains six admonishments to homosexuals and 362 admonishments to heterosexuals. That doesn't mean that God doesn't love heterosexuals. It's just that they need more supervision.
- Lynn Lavner, American comedian

If a bullet should enter my brain, let that bullet destroy every closet door.
- Harvey Milk, soon-to-be assassinated Mayor of San Francisco

When all Americans are treated as equal, no matter who they are or whom they love, we are all more free.
- Barack Obama, former President of the United States

This world would be a whole lot better if we just made an effort to be less horrible to one another.
- Elliot Page, actor and activist

I want to do the right thing and not hide anymore. I want to march for tolerance, acceptance, and understanding. I want to take a stand and say, "Me, too."
- Jason Collins, professional basketball player

Personally, coming out was one of the most important things I've ever done, lifting from my shoulders the millstone of lies that I hadn't even realized I was carrying.

- Sir Ian McKellan, English actor

So, make lots of noise. Kiss lots of boys. Or kiss lots of girls, if that's something you're into.

When the straight and narrow gets a little too straight, roll up a joint. Or don't.

Just follow your arrow wherever it points.

- Kacey Musgraves, in her song "Follow Your Arrow"

You can't just put gay in a little gay box anymore.

- Neil Patrick Harris, American actor

You can't plead tolerance for gays by saying that they're just like everyone else. Tolerance is something we should extend to people who are not like everyone else.

- Vito Russo, activist, film historian and author of the book "The Celluloid Closet"

We are made for goodness. We are made for love. We are made for friendliness. We are made for togetherness. We are made for all of the beautiful things that you and I know. We are made to tell the world that there are no outsiders. All are welcome: black, white, red, yellow, rich, poor, educated, not educated, male, female, gay, straight, all, all, all. We all belong to this family, this human family, God's family.

- Desmond Tutu, activist and Noble Peace Prize winner

You know, the matrix says, "Pick an identity and stick with it. Because I want to sell you some beer and shampoo and I need you to stick with what you are so I'll know how to market it to you.'" Drag is the opposite. Drag says, "Identity is a joke."

- RuPaul, the world's most famous drag queen

It's been a journey and a process of becoming totally out and sort of living that truth and having it be a daily thing. I'm at the point now that I want people to know that, and I want to talk about it. We're coming so far as a society, but we still have so far to go. So until we're all the way there, I'll probably die talking about it.

- Megan Rapinoe, professional soccer player and activist

Every gay and lesbian person who has been lucky enough to survive the turmoil of growing up is a survivor. Survivors always have an obligation to those who will face the same challenges.
- Bob Paris, author, activist, and former Mr. Universe

I was like, Am I gay? Am I straight? And I realized...I'm just slutty. Where's my parade?
- Margaret Cho, comedian

The next time someone asks you why LGBT Pride marches exist or why Gay Pride Month is June tell them "A bisexual woman named Brenda Howard thought it should be."
- Brenda Howard, activist and the "Mother of Pride"

If homosexuality is a disease, let's all call in queer to work: "Hello. Can't work today, still queer".
- Robyn Tyler, comedian

Homosexuality is God's way of ensuring that the truly gifted aren't burdened with children.
- Sam Austin, comedian, composer and lyricist

Before you criticize queens, fairies or someone who acts "too queer", consider where we'd be without them.
- Kenneth Hanes, American author

Nature made a mistake, which I have corrected.
- Christine Jorgensen, one of the first people to undergo gender confirmation surgery

I'm living by example by continuing on with my career and having a full, rich life, and I am incidentally gay.

- Portia DeRossi, Australian-American actress

What is straight? A line can be straight, or a street, but the human heart, oh, no, it's curved like a road through mountains.

- Tennessee Williams, American playwright in "A Streetcar Named Desire"

I think being gay is a blessing, and it's something I am thankful for every single day.

- Anderson Cooper, American journalist and host

The Lord is my Shepherd and he knows I'm gay.
-Troy Perry, founder of the Metropolitan Community Church

Yes, I wear foundation. Yes, I live with a man. Yes, I'm a middle- aged fag. But I know who I am, Val. It took me twenty years to get here, and I'm not gonna let some idiot senator destroy that. Fuck the senator, I don't give a damn what he thinks.
- Robin Williams as Armand in the movie, "The Birdcage"

Isn't it a violation of the Georgia sodomy law for the Supreme Court to have its head up its ass
- an anonymous letter to Playboy magazine in February 1987

I feel like I'm a boy, but I don't feel like I should've been born with different parts of my body or anything like that," she said. "I feel like it's just all in how I dress and how I talk and how I look and feel, and that makes me happy... I really sit in a more neutral place, which I'm grateful for as well.
- Ruby Rose, American actor

More guys should be bi.   It's 2018! It's like, get over yourselves!
- Kristen Bell as Eleanor Shellstrop on the television show, "The Good Place"

If you removed all of the homosexuals and homosexual influence from what is generally regarded as American culture, you would pretty much be left with "Let's Make a Deal.

- Fran Lebowitz, American author and social commentator

If God had wanted me otherwise, He would have created me otherwise.

- Johann von Goethe, German poet and playwright of the 18th and 19th Centuries

I know I'm perfectly as capable of being swayed by a girl as by a boy. More and more people feel that way, and I don't see why they shouldn't.

- Dusty Springfield, English popstar

Every person felt like they didn't belong, or at some point felt like they didn't need to carry on, they weren't needed. So I think it's important to show each other, "Look, we're all in this together, we all feel this way, let's work together.

- Cole Ledford, activist and social media influencer

Overall, the LGBT community, we're the same, we're like everybody else. Except we're better looking and more stylish.

- Wanda Sykes, American comedian and actress

No union is more profound than marriage, for it embodies the highest ideals of love, fidelity, devotion, sacrifice and family.
- Supreme Court Justice Anthony Kennedy's majority opinion in Obergefell vs. Hodges

These years in silence and reflection made me stronger and reminded me that acceptance has to come from within and that this kind of truth gives me the power to conquer emotions I didn't even know existed.
- Ricky Martin, Puerto Rican musical artist

Being gay is not a Western invention. It is a human reality.
- Hillary Clinton, American politician

Being gay is natural. Hating gay is a lifestyle choice.
- John Fugelsang, American host

I don't want you to love me. I don't want you to like me. But I don't want you to beat me up and kill me. You don't have to like me, I don't care. But please don't kill me.
- Kristin Beck, the first openly trans former US Navy Seal

We should indeed keep calm in the face of difference, and live our lives in a state of inclusion and wonder at the diversity of humanity.
- George Takei, actor and activist

I am a strong, black, lesbian woman. Every single time I say it, I feel so much better.

- Brittney Griner, professional basketball player

My voice is so high-pitched, only gay dogs can hear it.

- Ross Mathews, American television personality

I don't check any particular box. I've never caught feelings for anyone because they were a male or a female. I feel for people because of who they are. Not what they are.

- Tammy Ferebee, American author

I suppose it all began when I came out of the womb. I looked back up at my mother and thought to myself, "That's the last time I'm going up one of those."
- Stephen Fry, English actor and writer

I'm so gay, I could put a lisp in the word "cracker."
- Anthony 'Ant' Kalloniatis, American comedian and actor

Gay people don't actually try to convert people. That's Jehovah's Witnesses you're thinking of.
- Tina Fey, American humorist, writer and actress

Never be bullied into silence. Never allow yourself to be made a victim. Accept no one's definition of your life; define yourself.

- Harvey Fierstein, American actor, writer and activist

Gay Wit and Wisdom

If you enjoyed the list of quotes I've chosen, it would be mean the world to me if you would give us a good review. It'll only take a minute. Thank you so much.

And by way of a conclusion, I'd just like to add that these 100 quotations are just the beginning. I sifted through hundreds more pearls of wisdom. These are the ones that spoke to me, and I hope they speak to you as well.

And, of course the queer community is not a monolith. What is inspirational to one person, might seem dismissive to another. I particularly struggled with the Margaret Cho quote about bisexuality. To some it might be empowering. To others it might seen like a slight. Conversation is good, as long as we come from a place of mutual respect.

And it's worth noting that when you go in search of "queer inspirational quotes" or "funny gay mottos," you get a mixed bag. There are still a lot of people who don't believe in the ideals we share as a community. But, tides are changing... in large part due to the folks quoted in this book.

Thank you for your time.

47

Resources

9 Quotes to Inspire Action during Pride Month. (2019, June 10). Unfoundation.Org. https://unfoundation.org/blog/post/pride-month-quotes/

AIDS United. (2020, February 7). Inspiring HIV Quotes From Gay, Bi, Queer and SGL Black Leaders. POZ. https://www.poz.com/blog/inspiring-hiv-quotes-gay-bi-queer-sgl-black-leaders

Ballard, J. (2020, June 24). 25 Quotes From the LGBTQ+ Community to Help You Celebrate Pride and Learn About Its History. Woman's Day. https://www.womansday.com/life/g32858887/lgbtq-pride-quotes/

Brabaw, K. (2018, June 29). Let These 11 Powerful Quotes From LGBTQ+ Activists Sustain You Once Pride Month Ends. Refinery29. https://www.refinery29.com/en-us/lgbtq-motivational-quotes-from-gay-trans-activists

Careers, H. R. (2020, June 2). 20 Powerful LGBT Quotes that made history. Human Rights Careers. https://www.humanrightscareers.com/issues/lgbt-quotes/

Funny Gay Sayings and Funny Gay Quotes | Wise Sayings. (n.d.). WiseSayings.Com. https://www.wisesayings.com/funny-gay-quotes/

Funny quotes about GAY. (n.d.). FunnyComedianQuotes.Com. http://funnycomedianquotes.com/funny-quotes-and-jokes-about-gay.html?p=3

G. (n.d.). Humorous Gay Quotes | Gayest Store on Earth. GayestStoreOnEarth.Com. https://gayeststoreonearth.com/humorous-gay-quotes/

Gay Wit and Wisdom

Gattuso, R. (2020, June 16). 10 Inspiring Self-Love Quotes from LGBTQ Icons. Talkspace. https://www.talkspace.com/blog/inspiring-lgbtq-quotes-self-love/

Gay Quotes. (2021). BrainyQuote. https://www.brainyquote.com/topics/gay-quotes

Goldman, J. (2020, February 6). Celebrating Pride: 17 Powerful LGBT Quotes. Inc.Com. https://www.inc.com/jeremy-goldman/celebrating-pride-17-powerful-lgbt-quotes.html

Henderson, S. (2020, June 1). 14 Inspiring Quotes To Celebrate LGBT Pride Month — Because Love Is Love. YourTango. https://www.yourtango.com/2017303774/14-inspirational-lgbt-quotes-celebrate-pride-month

Hildreth, C. (2020, March 28). Powerful Pride: 10 Most Inspiring Quotes from LGBT Leaders. Cade Hildreth. https://cadehildreth.com/lgbt-leaders/

Inspirational quotes from 10 significant LGBTQI people in the Collection - National Portrait Gallery. (n.d.). Npr.Org.Uk. https://www.npg.org.uk/collections/lgbt-pride/

J., I. (2020, June 29). 8 Inspirational Gay and Lesbian Marriage Quotes. Love You Wedding. https://www.loveyouwedding.com/gay-and-lesbian-marriage-quotes/

Portal:LGBT/Random quote - Wikipedia. (2021). Wikipedia. https://en.wikipedia.org/wiki/Portal:LGBT/Random_quote

Q. (2018, October 1). 21 best LGBT quotes in honor of pride. Queer Culture Chats. https://queerculturechats.org/2018/06/04/21-best-lgbt-quotes-in-honor-of-pride/

Quotes about Homosexuality, Gay Rights, Pride, Sexual Orientation, Bisexuality, LGBTQ+, etc. (n.d.). QuoteGarden.Com. https://www.quotegarden.com/homosexuality.html

Rivero, N. R. (2020, June 9). 15 Inspiring Quotes from LGBTQ Leaders. Https://Www.Mentalfloss.Com/. https://www.mentalfloss.com/article/502121/inspiring-quotes-lgbtq-leaders

Search Results for "gay" –. (2021). Just-One-Liners.Com. https://www.just-one-liners.com/?s=gay

Sullivan, C. (2020, November 10). 11 Quotes About Coming Out From Non-Binary Celebrities That Are So Inspiring. Elite Daily. https://www.elitedaily.com/p/11-quotes-about-coming-out-from-non-binary-celebrities-that-are-so-inspiring-41708497

Teal, W. (2017, June 16). 15 Times Celebs Took a Powerful Stand for Marriage Equality. WeddingWire. https://www.weddingwire.com/wedding-ideas/gay-marriage-quotes

WBS Entertainment Co. (2020, June 12). 28 Great Quotes From LGBT Authors And Books. Worlds Best Story. https://worldsbeststory.com/blog/28-great-quotes-lgbt-authors-books/

Y. (2021, February 9). Best Inspirational Pride Month Quotes, Gay and LGBT Quotes. YourFates. https://www.yourfates.com/pride-month-quotes-gay-and-lgbt-quotes

Y. (2021b, February 9). Best Inspirational Pride Month Quotes, Gay and LGBT Quotes. YourFates. https://www.yourfates.com/pride-month-quotes-gay-and-lgbt-quotes/